BY-PATHS TO
THE PRESENCE OF GOD

BY-PATHS TO THE PRESENCE OF GOD

"MANE MECUM, DOMINE"

BY

S. M. BENVENUTA, O.S.D.

Catholic Authors Press
www.CatholicAuthors.com

Nihil obstat.
> GUALTERUS WELSH, S.T.D.,
> *Censor Deputatus.*

Imprimatur.
> ✠ JACOBUS AUGUSTINUS,
> *Archiep. S. And. et Ed.*

die 12 *Oct.* 1914.

First published by Sands & Co., 1914
Copyright 2007 Catholic Authors Press

ISBN: 0-9789432-7-9

Catholic Authors Press

Hartford, Connecticut

www.CatholicAuthors.org

PREFACE.

THIS little book will certainly effect much beauty.

People are the only means we have of finding out the meaning of the world; they are also perhaps the only means we have of finding out ourselves. Each artist, of whatever school, who tries to discover the meaning of beauty, succeeds just so far as he finds one single soul, real or ideal (whence he becomes a maker of realism or of romance), to unravel for him the tanglements of existence. It is indeed a reproach brought against the artist that in his pictures all the faces are the same. Yet surely that reproach must also be levelled against God, for He too made all things after One Only Figure: "In Him were made all things that were made." Still had the Creator no choice. He had to follow one only Type, for in It alone He found Infinite Beauty, and the Vision must needs spring to the Mind before the reality can come into Being. Man, therefore, who, in his creations, works but as an apprentice to the handicraft of God, must follow his Master's method of trade, and for good or ill find only in a personality the meaning of the world. Hence it is true that the faces in the artist's pictures are the same, for they are the face of the one who first taught him the meaning of life. Love is, of course, the great revealer, but we get at love through beauty, though ultimately beauty can only be explained by love.

But it is obvious that our view of the world will depend enormously upon the person who by beauty explains it to us. According as that figure approaches nearer and nearer to the Supreme Beauty, so is our understanding of life truer. As our phrase comes closer to the perfect utterance of God, which we call the Word, so ever more accurately do we read life's pages. Since all things were made by a Divine Personality, exist in Him, and were fashioned after His likeness, to find their richest and fullest meaning we must needs study them through the eyes of God.

Here this treatise on *By-Paths to the Presence of God* will help us. It gives us the whole of life in terms of Christ. It shows Him as the Beginning of all things and their perfect End. It tangles Him with the roots of the Universe, discovers him twin-made with all the world. The writer makes us realise in words of beauty that all life is sweet with a fragrant remembrance of Him: night with its companion sleep, food and drink, brambles and lilies, brooding hen and falling sparrow, hills and the sea, and boyhood.

Moreover, By-Paths have this advantage, that they are off the beaten track, that they are where one person alone has preceded us. They are narrow, of course, nor do they always turn in the way that we would have chosen. Yet are they thereby all the more interesting, for it is only the straight, broad road that leadeth to boredom.

BEDE JARRETT, *O.P.*

AUTHOR'S FOREWORD.

> "As one who came with ointments sweet,
> Abettors to her fleshy guilt,
> And brake and poured them at Thy Feet
> And worshipped Thee with spikenard spilt.
> So from a body full of blame,
> And tongue too deeply versed in shame,
> Do I pour speech upon Thy Name.
> Oh Thou, if tongue may yet beseech,
> Near to Thine awful feet let reach
> This broken spikenard of my speech."
> LAURENCE HOUSMAN.

THE following pages are the outcome of a line of thought suggested in a peculiarly helpful retreat. They were written in the diffident hope that in their turn they may prove suggestive to other religious souls. In many cases the ideas are but half thoughts, so imperfectly are they developed. The writer has not tried to complete them, feeling that those thoughts which we ourselves develop are the most potent, the most productive of action. If thought is not productive of outer works of some sort then its influence is baneful. It leaves us merely sentimentalists. Again, it may be objected that many of the thoughts are mere queries. Such, if examined, will be found to deal with subjects where positive assertion would be utter presumption, yet, with subjects which lure the mind to speculation ;—who amongst us does not wonder at times what God's thoughts are on many of the questions that worry us here below, and who has not felt his own wonder itself to be an answer of some sort even though He could not put that answer into words.

"Mane Mecum, Domine."
By-Paths to the Presence of God.

"WHOM seek ye?"

And they answered Him: "Jesus of Nazareth."

You remember the scene: the garden where the moon sent its splintered arrows of silver radiance athwart the twisted olive boughs, the broken figure of the Man of Sorrows as he staggered to His feet and went forward to meet His foes, the little band of disciples, shrinking yet eager, the clean-shaven, impassive faces of the soldiers, the Jewish rabble, hatred lighting up their dark eyes, Judas with the flagrant kiss of the Saviour fresh upon his sin-blistered lips, "Whom seek ye?"

Look into His Heart as He puts the

question, as He hears the answer from those throats of brass. Look, at least as far as human eyes can fathom, for though there are unplumbed divine deeps within the Heart of the Man-God there are human shallows too. Did He not prove this to us once for all when in the Pharisee's house He numbered the slights put upon Him. He felt them as only a sensitive human being could, even though at that very moment the Angels veiled their faces in lowliest adoration of His Godhead, even though His Mother's silent worship spake louder than aught else in creation, even though the Magdalen's tears were warm upon His sacred feet. " *Thou* gavest me no kiss." . . .

" *Whom* seek ye ? " Men of Juda, I have cleansed you of your leprosy, I have raised your dead to life, I have fed you when ye hungered in the wilderness. I have blessed your little children, I have wept for you, I have bled for you, My heart is even now bursting for love of you, yea, for such as you.

" Whom seek ye ? "

And they answered Him: "Jesus of Nazareth."

Why they sought Him He well knew. Think how those words fell upon His Divine Ear: how they mocked the love in His Heart for each individual actor in that garden drama. A little while before His Father had sent an Angel to comfort his dire distress, to brace the Will, stretched, humanly speaking, to snapping point beneath the weight of the world's sin. What comfort did the Father's messenger bring that should nerve Him here to meet this tide of unrequited love? Did he gently bid Our Lord pierce the shadowy veil of the Future, did the Angel point down the ages to young faces and old, fair faces and faces unlovely in the world's dull eyes, to eager faces and faces chastened by the kiss of Patience, the sad-eyed, all turned with a look of deep desire towards "The Scarlet Figure of History?"

"Whom seek ye?"

And they answered Him: "Jesus of Nazareth."

Let the answer ring out far and wide across the gulf of Time even to the sea of Eternity. Let the fair hills of Love repeat the echo from their hollow places!

"Whom seek ye?"

And they answered Him: "Jesus of Nazareth."

．　．　．　．　．

The practice of the Presence of God is indispensable to seekers after Christ. It is old as humanity; Adam walked with God. It is fresh as its perennial source, which is Love. Augustine, whom the whole world loves, for it ever loves a lover, found therein a source to slake his human craving for love and companionship, and Faber, in characteristically tender accents, calls out "There is nothing in life one half so sweet as to think of God." Saint Teresa teaches us how to practice this exercise by considering God, or as she would quaintly put it, "His Majesty," not without us, not above us, not far away from any one of us, but within our very souls waiting for us to turn to Him. How old the doctrine is : "In Him we live and move and have our being." I sought Him without and lo, He was within me: so Paul and Augustine. Saint Catherine of Siena tells us when they took her little room from her that she might be forced to give up her prayer, she found " Him in the little cell of Her own heart." How human it all is. Just as we love to catch the tones, to repeat the words of our loved ones—sometimes we do it unconsciously—so the Friends of the Saviour, great and small, wittingly or unwittingly, at times in clear trumpet notes, again in the faltering stammering lisp of spiritual childhood, echoed the Master's own words, " The Kingdom of God is within you." Ah yes, it is sweet indeed to think of God, comforting to feel the clasp of His strong arm, inebriating to catch the secret music of His words spoken in the deep of our own heart. But we weaker souls forget at times. We leave Him waiting alone in the Inmost Chamber of the Castle while we walk abroad. There is no word of reproach on His lips when we come back, but the love of

His lovely eyes is a thorn to pierce us with.
"Thou woundest with a thorn of light." Why
have we left Him alone waiting? There is to
the world always a something slightly ridiculous
in the lover who is waiting at the trysting place.
To truer and more sensitive minds he is not
ridiculous, only pathetic, with the soul hunger
in his eyes. And we keep *Him* waiting in
our hearts, ah, so often. We cannot help it.
We are men, not disembodied spirits. We
must eat and drink, rise up and lie down
again, marry and give in marriage, and all
these things distract us. True, but what if
we used these very things to bring us closer
to our Lord, if each was to us a memorial of
Him: if we saw Him in each other's eyes,
caught the echo of His tones, albeit at times
distorted, but still an echo in each other's
speech—ah, what then! Soon would we grow
like the white-robed mediæval mystic of
Cologne, Blessed Henry Suso, of whom men
said that he was as one who lived with Christ.
" Jesus always seemed so visibly present to
his mind that he was as one who walked in

the body by Our Lord's side, even in the smallest action." If he ate it was with Christ and His Apostles, if he drank, if he slept, if he preached, if he studied, if he taught he turned to Jesus as the lodestone to the pole. "Once at least in his life each man walks with Christ to Emmaus," not merely to Emmaus. If we will we can walk with Him, though at times our eyes be held, every step of the journey from Time to Eternity, we can follow the stripling stream of life from its mountain source till, a mighty river, it rushes swift and silent under the mysterious shadows of the dark pines of the valley of death out, out, to lose itself in the sea. "If thou wouldst." It is not so very hard. Let us try for a little while at least, asking Him always to hold us by the hand, to lead us whithersoever He would, and see if Faber's words do not become to us more meaningful. "There is nothing in life one half so sweet as to think of God."

. . . . .

Let us consider awhile the daily duties of life and some of its joys too. If we are

Christians at all, sorrow brings us closer to the Man of Sorrows. "The waters of sad knowledge leave their inevitable delta on the soul."[1] Sorrow, like the sacred river of the Egyptians, clothes with hopeful verdure the arid wastes of many a life, but joy? Yet joy too is a creature of God and should lead us to Him. Christ brightened by His sunshine presence the marriage feast of Cana. Think what that meant. The guests that are bidden to a wedding feast may be divided into two classes: those whom the young couple ask because they must, and those they ask because they would. The first may cloud the feast. The young bride's thoughts may be torn from the bridegroom lest the exacting guest whom duty or interest bids her honour may see some fancied slight at her table. She is uneasy all the time he tarries at her house. It is so easy to offend him, so hard to please, and in his hands he weilds the power to advance or hinder the fortunes of her beloved. If she can see him

[1] Francis Thompson.

safely out of the house she will breathe freer. Then there is the love-bidden guest. Joy is more radiant when his eyes reflect its sparkle, the thousand little nothings, the every day courtesies of life, take on a new meaning when he is there. His are the gifts, trivial though they be in other's eyes, of which the bride truly says, "No gift is ever little." Ah, you know the guest! Such a guest Jesus must have been to that young couple of Cana. They must have loved Him in His human capacity not yet knowing Him as the Son of God. They were poor and could not be lavish with their invitations. There could not possibly have been any interested reason for bidding Him to their board. He was too poor, too unimportant. My God, too unimportant! . . . So they asked Him that their joy might be more full for His being there. And He came to do their bidding. Surely then as now the wedding guests uttered loving wishes for the newly married pair; said sweet, tender, foolish things about their future. What did Jesus say? What wish that brought its own fulfilment sped from His human heart? Ah Saint John! Saint John! "But there are also many other things which Jesus did which, if they were written, every one, the world itself, I think, would not be able to contain the books that should be written." . . . When we are bidden to some festive board, instead of accepting the invitation as an inevitable bit of dissipation, can we not go in company with the Divine Wedding Guest? We can ask Him to whisper in our ear from time to time as we pass His gifts to one another. We can spare a smile or two now and again from our fellow guests to speed to Him alone. Lessing, the German dramatist, puts into the mouth of Minna Von Barnhelm a little phrase that we can make our own: "The truest prayer to the Creator is a grateful look towards Heaven." This appearance of Jesus at Cana was nothing foreign to His character. We see Him bidden, though not by love, to the feasts of the Pharisees, we see Him share too Peter's humble meal after curing His Apostle's mother-in-law, " And she rose and ministered to Him." How eager the old woman must have been to serve Him, how the old knotted hands must have trembled in their eagerness as she placed her poor best before the all-indulgent Christ. Think of the sweet, old face, wrinkled and careworn—life is always hard for the poor—of the dark Jewish eyes, dim with gratitude's unshed tears as spellbound she watched the Saviour break bread with Peter. Surely the memory of these things can help us to sanctify the little courtesies of life, can teach us to share with Him its common every day joys. "Give me wisdom that she may be with me," that she may teach me to find You in all my ways.

. . . . .

We go to rest each night. How full the night is of Him, the night when He loved to go up into the silent mountains to pray. We divest ourselves of the raiment of the day ; we can think of Him when, as a child, tenderly and reverently Mary undressed Him, every touch a caress, and all the while those dark

Eyes of Wisdom looked up at her with a strange light in their depths. A time would come, ah, well the Child God knew it, when for Him there would be another unrobing, when shame alone would cover Him as a garment. And Mary? Mary pondered many things in her heart. How much she knew or how much He mercifully held back from her we know not. Of this, at least, we may be sure. She knew every prophecy that referred to Him, so that David's words must often have been in her mind as she undressed Him for the night. "Upon my vesture they have cast lots." Who were "they"? Why should they cast lots upon His vesture, that seamless robe into which every thread had been woven by maternal and, literally, adoring hands? Did the question falter on her lips, did she check its utterance, content to know only those things that He would tell her of His own accord? Then when she smoothed the silken curls she would remember the reference to the diadem wherewith His mother had crowned Him. Surely in the early days at least happily she knew not what this meant. The diadem? Truly Mother that little Head will be crowned with a diadem, but not of gold, that were all too base. No precious stone will shine above His brow; the lustre of His Eyes would shame its borrowed fires. Crowned will He be, yea, with that alone wherewith no other king was ever crowned, even with a circlet of spine. Jesus of Nazareth, *King* of the Jews, have mercy on us!

"These are trivial things to single out of Christ's life for food of thought. Let us dwell rather on the larger issues." Is anything trivial in the life of Christ? We put different actions in different categories and label them great and small. Maybe "on the hither side" the labels will be reversed, maybe that looking back we shall see that the deep things of life lay very close to its uttermost simplicities. Our Blessed Lady we know was the deepest of all contemplatives. Immeasurably above and beyond the flight of highest saint or fire-touched seraph was the flight of her pure soul into the infinite spaces of the Godhead, yet for long years the object of her rapturous contemplation was not the Wonder-Worker of Galilee, not the Man-God in the blaze of His Divinity on Thabor, nor in the still more deific light of Calvary's darkness, but the Child-God, the Boy-God in the daily acts that His humanity necessitated. Abyss calleth to abyss; from infinite strength to the frailty of babyhood Mary's spirit turned; from her Child's weakness she learned the Omnipotence of His Love. In divine as in human truths the juxtaposition of extremes drives home a lesson more effectually than a separate study of either.

" God's Fair were guessed scarce but for opposite sin
Yea, and His Mercy, I do think it well,
Is flashed back from the brazen gate of Hell.
        The heavens decree
All power fulfil itself as soul in thee,
For supreme Spirit subject was to-day
And Law from its own servants learned a law
And Light besought a lamp unto its way,
        And Awe was reined in awe
        At one small house of Nazareth." [1]

[1] Francis Thompson.

Holy Mary, Mother of God, pray for us sinners *now*, that our contemplation too may be fruitful, and at the hour of our death.

Amen.

Or we may think of Him in His manhood, just before His mission began, for after that we know He had not whereon to lay His Head. Under the roof-tree of Nazareth he was one of the sons of men. There he divested Himself of His garments before He went to rest, too old now for mother love to minister to Him. How He would have folded each garment ere He laid it aside. Was that why Saint John in his beautiful Resurrection gospel tells us "Simeon Peter . . . saw the linen cloths lying and the napkin that had been about His head . . . *wrapt in one place*"? We can fancy those early Christians who had known Him personally pause over these lines and, as they raised tear-dimmed eyes the one to the other, whisper softly: "It was so like the Master, was it not; folded garments." There must be many a little touch about His life story that went straight to their hearts, touches which are lost on us whose knowledge of Him is so much inferior to theirs. Keen and loving study of the Gospel would surely reveal some of these to us. Whisper to us, dearest Lord, when with dull, childish, uncomprehending eyes we read such, for we too would fain discover traits infinitely characteristic of Thee, small traits that are memorable to love. The larger ones even our dull wits can comprehend. " Domine ut videamus."

.   .   .   .   .

When we lie down to rest we can think of Him when He lay sleeping. Perhaps we picture Him, the little Babe upon His mother's breast. Would that we could fathom the least shallow of the tide of deep calm love and lowly worship of her high thoughts as His tiny heart lay beating over hers—shallow that were high-water mark for any thought of ours to reach. We can see her too kneeling before His crib absorbed in adoring contemplation. What she thought, what she said we knew not, but we can unite our silence to that high speech of hers. Later on He was a beautiful boy, growing in age and grace, Our Blessed Lady must surely in the fashion of mothers the wide world over . . . . His divinity did not rob her motherhood of its humanity . . . . have often stolen in at night to look down upon the Son of God, who was also her own little Son, while He slept. Gently might she have brushed aside the silken curls to mark the lovely flush of sleeping childhood on the softly rounded cheek that lay pillowed in the finely shaped, slender, brown hand. He slept too in the open even as a child—not on the road to Egypt, for there had He not the red pavilion of Mary's heart, canopy the most worthy earth could offer?—but when as a boy of twelve He was houseless in the streets of Jerusalem. They tell us that He then slept in the porch of the temple. Look down upon Him there; see the beautiful contour of His young form, half revealed, half concealed by the graceful Eastern garments, the boyish head supported by some step or marble pillar, cold resting place for love; the long silken lashes resting on the olive cheek, the red sensitive lips parted, the hot breath of the life of God passing through them. Did no Jewish mother pass by the way, catch sight of the touching figure in the soft light of the Pascal moon or under the gentler radiance of the stars, and carry Him in to her home, or were the houses of the thronged city so full of guests that again there was no room for Him? We do not know; we cannot tell. Ah, shall we not question Him on the mystery of those three days in the long Eternity that lies before us! There will be then no need for Evangelist to record "And Jesus answering said to them," for we ourselves shall keep the record in our hearts.

Again we may see the young prophet of Nazareth, wearied out after the toilsome labours of a full day, resting His Head against a brown coil of rope, stretched in some corner of a little fishing smack. Surely some Apostle's eyes travelled down hither

from the nets now and again, or some back
that was bent wearily over the plashing oars,
some strained figure lashing together the dun
hempen sail, straightened itself so that a pair
of loving eyes might rest awhile on His pure,
sweet face. Perchance too, as the breeze
freshened and the night dew began to fall
chilly, John divested himself of his outward
garment and laid it softly, oh so softly, across
the sleeping figure.

> Hush ! the Master sleepeth at the prow,
> The day was long, He is awearied now.
> The fisher-folk in silence hold their breath
> Lest they should wake Him from that trance like death.
> John crept adown the boat. A little space
> He stood agazing down on Jesus' face.
> White misty moonbeams fell on brow and chin.
> Then sudden mindful of the Soul within
> Which slumb'ring slept not, on his knees he fell
> And Jesus worshipped long and full and well.

Ere we close our own tired eyes, with John
we can gaze upon that sleeping form, with John

we can wonder, holding our breath in awe, where was the soul of Christ, Our Lord, the while His Body lay unconscious. Did the grave eyes smile beneath their lidded veil at the attitude His seeming unconsciousness made His friends assume in spite of their first vague apprehensions of His Divinity, or was His Soul treading the yawning chasm of Space, speeding, swift as the lightning flash, to the Bosom of the Father? Soul of Christ, sanctify me! Keep us, O Lord, that we may rest in Christ and sleep in peace!

.   .   .   .   .

We eat and drink. Here too we may find Him if we will, and that too not merely like that sweet boy mystic of Father Benson's who ever needs must break his food into five portions in remembrance of His Lord's Five Wounds. We can rejoice to partake of those very foods that once crossed His blessed lips. It is a foolish, childish thing of which to make a joy, but when was love ever wise? Even if He Himself should smile thereat may we not look up boldly and ask with the Seraph of Assisi:—

> "Was that love wise, Oh Saviour Mine,
> Which drew Thee down to earth below?
>
> .   .   .   .   .   .
>
> This love which makes me foolish, lo !
> It took away Thy Wisdom quite :
> This love which makes me languish so
> It took away Thy very Might."

"Ah yes," the timid soul may reply, "but Saint Francis was a saint, a very seraph. He could aspire to such love with such and greater excesses, but I—who am I that I should offer to God my pityful attempts at love ? Practices such as these are for the saints, for those who have served God whole-heartedly from their youth. Let such as these pour out their unsullied treasures over His feet. As for me, who dare not aspire so high, let me remember my sins and keep the fear of God ever before me."

And yet, beloved, His call, nay His *command*, is in our ears, even in yours and mine.

"He does not want *my* personal love. I would I could believe He did. It would make life so much easier, so much sweeter."

Listen, beloved : *Thou* shalt love the Lord Thy God, with thy whole heart, with thy whole soul, with all thy strength, with all thy mind. *Thou* shalt. It is a personal command to me, to you. Men love with their minds, women with their hearts. The love of each is in some sort maimed. The love here commanded is to be without blemish, to be complete. We may well ask ourselves, you and I, where we shall get such love that we may simply do what we have been commanded. "Lord, to whom shall we go but to Thee?" Let us with gentle violence remind Thee of the night Thou madest—if in loving reverence we dare call it so—the one sweet boast of Thy life—"the Father loveth me because I ever do the things which please Him." Here then, dearest Lord, is something which pleases the Father. He asks me, even me, for my heart. Without Thee I cannot give it Him, not even now at the eleventh hour. Please the Father then in this, dear Lord, by enabling me to love Him with my whole heart, fix my wayward feelings on Him; with my whole soul, make all my faculties His, draw out for His glory all the possibilities of this nature that thou hast given me, with all my strength, make me generous that I may use it for Him till the last, with all my mind, that it may be fired with longing to know Him more and more.

> "Lord, when my heart was whole I kept it back
> And grudged to give it Thee,
> Now then that it is broken, must I lack
> Thy kind word 'Give it me?'
> Silence would be but just, and Thou art just,
> Yet since I lie here scattered in the dust,
> With still an eye to lift to Thee,
> A broken heart to give
> I think that Thou wilt bade me live
> And answer 'Give it Me.'"[1]

. . . . .

Jesus drank. What did He drink? Our daily beverages differ much from those of

[1] Christina Rossetti.

the Eastern two thousand years ago. But some liquids we share with them. We drink water and we drink wine as they did. Water! Is water sacred in the eyes of the Creator? It would seem as if He has a special predilection for this inanimate creature of His. He made it priest-like to lave away the sordid stains of common life. He willed it to be used in the keystone sacrament of His system, the laver of regeneration. Christ was poor. Water was then possibly His ordinary drink, this same crystal liquid that passes your lips and mine, beloved. In the Old Testament we find a prophecy relating to the drinking of water by Christ, "He shall drink of the brook by the way" Catherine Emmerich tells us this was fulfilled when on that night of bitter woe they hurled Him headlong into the brook Cedron on their rapid march towards the darkened city. This may well be so, for Christ we know "was the denial as well as the fulfilment of every prophecy" denial, in the sense that He deceived the human hopes built upon them by those who

interpret prophecies after the desires of their
own heart. Here the prophecy would be fulfilled to the letter, yet in its bitter irony would
rankle in our hearts almost as a denial. Still,
experience shows us that with God there is a
strange simplicity too about the way in which
prophecies are fulfilled. Surely during His
sojourn in the desert or on His many unrecorded marches through Palestine, Christ
must have often knelt by some bank o'ergrown with creepers and, catching the running
waters of some mountain Wady in the hollow
of His hand, so have quenched His thirst
even as His poorer brethren do unto this day.
As His sacred fingers touched the cooling
tide, looking afar out, with eyes that knew no
limit of time or space, He would see the blue
mountain lake on whose bosom He was later
to preach to the multitude that lined its
shelving shore; see Peter on the shingly
beach mending the nets, all unconscious of
the destiny that lay before him, his narrow
horizon bounded by the low hills that circled
the sea of Galilee, the same Peter who in after

years was to pray Christ to bid him walk
upon those self same waters. Not to earth
alone did the eyes of the Man-God travel.
The water that spent itself so lavishly in its
hollow bed would bid Him look across the
great chasm to see Dives buried in hell; bid
the divine ear hear those tortured lips call out
for one little drop of water.

> "Such spilt water as in dreams must cheat
> The undying throats of Hell athirst alway."[1]

What were our Master's thoughts at such
sights as this? Above us, beyond us, as
high as are the heavens above the earth we
know they were but surely as the crystal
drops of the stream trickled from His fingers,
slow and heavy as the first of a thunder
shower He saw through the gathering darkness of Golgotha the Centurion raise his
spear, "And immediately there came out
blood and water," slow, heavy tears of Christ's
broken heart, tears that availed naught to

[1] Dante Gabriel Rossetti.

save the sinners whom He loved. "Water issuing from the side of Christ, wash me!"

Christ drank wine too. They taunted Him as "a wine-bibber," weaving into the warp and woof of falsehood that one slight thread of truth. John came drinking no wine and they would have none of him. Jesus came and hallowed the wine cup with His blessed lips, and lo, they tried to turn the hallowing into a desecration. How solemn must have been the thoughts of Christ as He lifted to His lips the grape juice that one day He was to change into His Own Precious Blood. Not at the Last Supper alone did He ponder on this mystery. As a child in Nazareth, when He sat by the door on summer evenings with the clinging vine tendrils turned in the lattice work above His head, did His baby fingers bless the juice within those purple and amber clusters? Francis Thompson compares a child to a grape

"Whose veins ran snow instead of wine."

The Boy-Poet of Nazareth saw in the womb

of the future that sacred vine whose veins ran Blood. "Blood of Christ, inebriate me!" He cursed a fig tree once: why then should He not have blessed this other fruit tree, which typified His Own fair self, with its luxuriant branches, some clinging close to the parent stem and others trailing afar in riotous confusion, branches emblematic of you and of me? As Mary sat spinning, turning her wheel with silver din, ever and anon resting her eyes upon that lovely Child form fondly fingering the vine leaves, the anticipation of the day when at her gentle bidding He would turn the crystal water into wine, Blood-red, must have risen before His mind. Those grapes too would have spoken to Him of the bitter potion His dying lips were to taste, vinegar, that is, wine fermented. Ah, how bitter is the potion you offer to my dying lips, O vine, for whom I shed my heart's blood, Sitio, I thirst, "I planted thee a most beautiful vine: and thou hast proved exceeding bitter to me: for in my thirst thou gavest me vinegar to drink."

> Oh Jesus, who for love of me
> Did'st agonise on Calvary,
> In Thy sweet mercy grant to me
> To suffer and to die for Thee.

.   .   .   .   .

Of the foods we eat which are those of which the Son of God in His mortal life partook? Food varies with nationality, with climate, with the age in which we live, with the social circle within which we move. Christ was a Jew who lived in a semi-tropical climate nigh two thousand years ago. He was but a poor carpenter, so His fare was possibly humbler than that to which we are accustomed. Still there are foods which are of all times and of all places and conditions. When we partake of these we can please ourselves with the thought that we are sharing in a more particular way Christ's daily fare. Bread was the staff of life to Him even as it is to us. As He broke it in His holy fingers what anticipative memories must have crowded round His heart and brain; the few barley loaves He was to multiply to feed the thousand; the day when sitting upon a knoll covered with grass:—did Christ specially love grass, and if so, was it that to the Oriental those sword shaped strips of fluted green brought a joy which surfeited eyes like ours can never know, or was it the Artist in Him that loved the red brown earth with its glorious enamel of meadow grass; thoughts such as these inevitably suggest themselves as we read the Evangelist's words, which in their quaint simplicity make us wonder why they were recorded in the sublime pages of the Gospel, " and there was much grass about the place,"—that day when, as He sat upon the gentle eminence with far below the calm sun-kissed lake, circled by the sloping shores where the fields were white to the harvest, the earnest little band of simple fisher folk should bid Him teach them how to pray, and as He raised those wonderful eyes of His to " Our Father who art in Heaven," the petition fell from lips divine, " Give us this day our daily dread." Did the tender curves of His lips soften into a wistful smile as anticipatively He saw the literal, childish way His disciples would echo this petition. They would think alone of the meat that perisheth. He would patiently bide His time till He had reared them to higher stature, when He would reveal the secret of the King. He would think too of the time when He would hand a piece of bread dipped to Judas the traitor, Judas the well loved apostle; Love's heart rending but futile appeal; to His betrayer; of the time when He would give them His body instead of bread. Had Christ a strange reverential way of handling bread; may that be one of the reasons why the disciples of Emmaus "knew Him in the breaking of bread"? Well may we ask but who shall answer us? "Lord to whom shall we go but to Thee. Give us always this bread."

Bread is corn, *bruised*, surely the Living Bread was ground as very corn "for us men and for our salvation." "Unless the grain of wheat die and be buried in the earth" . . . . "Give us this day our daily superstantial bread, Our Father who art in Heaven, give it to us, Father, through Jesus Christ Our Lord, Amen."

Fish was another food which must often have crossed the Master's lips, for He shared the poor fare of His apostles. During this early apostleship at least they did not abandon their craft, so that fish would naturally at this time have formed a staple part of their diet and His. Christ worked many miracles through this medium, multiplying the few fishes in the desert, giving the fishers the miraculous draught, bidding Peter take the stater from the mouth of the fish. Even in His risen life He partook of their meal of fish and honeycomb to prove to them the substantiality of His glorified body. Most touching of all is the description of the meal He prepared for them on the lake-shore in the " first white peep of dawn that is neither light nor darkness. He was there lonely in the dark, the same Christ they had left lonely in the hands of His enemies, yet so different in His glorified humanity. Oh, but His heart was unchanged, they knew that as they saw

Him standing by the embers that glowed red. "They saw hot coals lying and a fish laid thereon and bread." The tender love of Christ! Was He not Father and Mother as well as brother and friend. They had failed Him in His sorest need, and He—He was there to wait upon their needs. "Though thou shouldst slay me I will not let thee go! We have slain *Thee*, Lamb of God, but oh, for all that, nay, *verily for that*, slacken not Thy hold upon us."

> "Christ by Thine our darkened hour,
> Live within my heart and brain
> Let my hands not slip the rein.
>
> Ah how long ago it is
> Since a comrade rode with me!
> Now a moment let me see
> 'Thyself, lonely in the dark
> Perfect, without wound or mark.'" [1]

There are other common foods which Christ once ate, such as butter and honey. We are sure of these two, "butter and honey shall He eat." The prophecy is undoubtedly

[1] Padraic Column.

symbolic, but as we saw before Christ had a way of fulfilling prophecies literally with all the simplicity of true majesty. Before Him John ate locusts and wild honey. In Nazareth Our Blessed Lady would perhaps in mother fashion deny herself some necessary that she might purchase for Her Boy some simple delicacy such as honey or butter, for butter is a delicacy to the poor, even the decent working poor, and Jesus, in a most unboyish fashion, would have insisted on His mother and foster father sharing the luxury, too small to be divided by any save by the magnifying hands of love. He ate butter then and honey, and in all probability cheese too. Then there were the fruits which we share with Him, figs, not brown, dried seed-bags such as we know, but the plump, soft green fruits familiar to our neighbours of the South; apples, a fruit which seems to have a symbolic value in Palestine, if we consider the many references to it made in the Old Testament, starting with that golden fruit that grew upon the Tree of Knowledge; olives, ah the bitter sweet thoughts that small fruit would have called up in the Saviour's breast, as He sat at the hospitably spread board in Bethany, or passed some hill-side orchard covered with its silver grey foliage. "Do you remember the look that used to come into the Master's eyes—the same that always lit His face whenever pain of any sort touched Him personally—the look He always had when He passed the olive boughs," we can well fancy some of His disciples to have said talking over the Master's ways long years after His Ascension. "Little did we then think it was of the garden where, alone, He endured that sweat of Blood they reminded Him. How blind we were in the old days, ah, how very blind!"

.   .   .   .   .

"What symbolism is this with more food! Is it fantastic!" If it be so, beloved, we have fair precedence for our phantasy. Did not *He* point to the tiny glistening crystals with which we too season our food and say, "Ye are the salt of the earth!" Let us then hallow our food with memories of Him. "Whether you eat or whether you drink or whatever else you do, do all for the glory of God."

. . . . .

As we go in and out of doors we find so much to remind us of the Master. Chesterton in one of his books describes a French atheist whom hatred for all things concerning Christ had driven mad. This man once walking home broke into a fit of ungovernable passion, wreaking vengeance on every common object that crossed his path. The cement on the paving stones was conspiring against him for it showed crosses beneath his feet; the railings of the houses angered him for they were crosses too. In his terrible anger against the Cross of Christ, the man wrecked all around him until at last his friends were forced to take his freedom from him. What Hate, the Destroyer, did for this man could not Love, the Regenerator, do for you and me, beloved? As we pass through a doorway we can see as He must have seen, how the panels of the door form a cross, shadow of the Cross whereon He was to die. When as a child He looked up at night into the dark vault of Heaven with its myriad twinkling stars—the same golden orbs that we see now—when He caught sight of Orion's flashing belt it may well have been to Him a cross blazoned in the midnight sky. Well may He have looked down the labyrinthine years, the tangled twisted years from then till now, and seen the touching figures of that white haired father and his little daughter, "treading the skirts of eventide," seen the delight mirrored in the child's brown eyes as rapturously she raised them heavenwards. "See papa, my name is written in heaven." True, Little Flower, flashes gem like in the quiet sky, but it is His Cross as well as Thy name.

He could trace the Cross in the simple household furniture; rafters are laid crosswise. The frames of the little windows in Nazareth showed the Cross, the lintel of the door, nay, the very road that led down from the little village among the hills was soon intersected by another path and the two formed a cross. He was the Way but the Way stretched cross-wise. The branches of the wayside trees spread out as the arms of a cross as if to bid Him turn His gaze to that other tree on which He was to hang. How long did that tree take to grow from which Christ's Cross was to be made; did the seed fall into the brown upturned earth that April morn on which Gabriel brought tidings of great joy to Mary; did it like His seamless robe grow with His growth, tall, straight and unblemished, fit stem for the fairest fruit on earth to be grafted on? The cross was here, was there, was everywhere for him who had eyes to see.

"Who can deny me power and liberty
To stretch mine arms and mine own cross to be?
Swim and at every stroke thou art thy cross.
The mast and yard make one where seas do toss.
Look down, thou spiest our crosses in small things:
Look up, thou seest birds raised on cross wings."[1]

[1] Donne.

Our Blessed Lady's habitual outlook on these common things must have been tinged by some such thought as this, at least from the time He first told her the Son of Man must go up to Jerusalem to be crucified. Holman Hunt in, "The Shadow of the Cross" portrays some such incident in Nazareth. His picture shows our Lady starting at the Shadow of the Cross thrown upon the wall from the figure of Our Blessed Lord.

> "That Shadow dear upon the wall,
>   Where level rays of evening fall,
>   And bid us view the Lord uprear
>   His tired arms in the sunset clear—
>   Let it console us, not appal.
>   That Shadow has a voice for all
>   Whom other Shadows may enthral:
>   It soothes away our mortal fear,
>   That Shadow dear.
>   Invite its presence, hear its call,
>   Dwellers in cottage or in hall.
>   Rest not until the sign appear,
>   Then sit beneath it all the year;
>   It whispers peace, whate'er befal—
>   That Shadow dear."

The brambles in the ditches with their profusion of cruel thorns told similar tales to Him. What were the thoughts of the Boy of Nazareth when He marked these long, slender but sturdy spears, with their points cunningly turned downwards the more cruelly to tear unresisting flesh: did He ever gather them in His soft young hands to try how much they hurt: did Mary find the little hands bleeding and gently take the brambles from Him, the question on her lips checked by the intensity of His youthful glance? Do no thoughts such as these arise within *us* at the sight of bramble bushes?

> "Earth's crammed with heaven,
> And every common bush afire with God;
> But only he who sees takes off his shoes;
> The rest sit round it, and pick blackberries." [1]

．　　　．　　　．　　　．　　　．

The earth is changed since His footsteps once blessed it, aye, much changed, but still there are some features which scarce have felt time's impress. The sun still sinks to his

[1] Elizabeth Barrett Browning.

western rest a blaze of purple and crimson, amethyst and gold. How often did His divine eyes rest on it with all an artist's delight in the gorgeous riot of colour, how often too with the simple eye of peasant wisdom which knows that when "in the evening the sky is red, the morrow will be fair."

The hills are round about us, those

> "Summits, lone and high,
> That traffic with the eternal sky."[1]

Hills and the sea team with memories of Him. His childhood's home was in among the hills. Amid the bustle of His public life He loved to retire into a mountain alone to pray. Standing with the Twelve at the foot of some hill we can watch the tall, white robed figure of the young Prophet climb its brow, watch Him till the darkness closes round about Him and hides Him from our gaze. We can wonder what His thoughts are, what His words to His Heavenly Father through the

[1] William Watson.

long watches of the night when unawed He heard

> "the everlasting fingers ply
> The loom of God."

The storm-tossed seas still lash our shores: the mountain torrents still tumble headlong into tarns: then as now the streamlets babble over their pebble-strewn beds. His divine eyes must often have rested on the "wine-dark" shores of the Mediterranean, caught from some vantage point on one of the northern hills of Judea. Did imagination conjure up for Him the far-off murmur of its ebb and flow, a murmur laden with the eternal note of sadness, or did minor chords of poor broken human lives make Him deaf to these waiting cadences of Nature? It cannot be so. It is the materialist philanthropist who is too busy healing the bodies of men to have time to lift his gaze for one brief moment beyond their sores and bruises to the lovely sights of Nature's other children, to lend his ears to the music of their sounds. The eyes that rested undazzled upon the white splendours of the Beatific Vision kindled in admiration at the flaming glories of "a lily of the field," so in fancy we can see the Master straining His gaze towards the west where the sunlight danced upon those rippling waters, the fresh mountain breezes lifting the Nazarene's long hair from off the noble brow, the hand raised to shade the eyes that darkened with the long thoughts of anticipative love. His heart went out to each of us, even to you and me, beloved, as He saw the billows rage and the winds howl round our frail crafts, the old reproach upon our lips: "Lord, save us! We perish!" Peter said once to Him, "Lord, Thou knowest all things." He is Jesus Christ, the same yesterday, to-day, for ever. He knew, He knows our storms, our doubts, our fears, our meannesses that we scarce half own even to ourselves. "Lord, save us! We perish!"

Rivers hold sweet memories of Christ for us. It was in the river Jordan, the same in which the leper Naaman had been cleansed of his leprosy and his skin made as the skin of a little child, that Jesus stood in exquisite humility to receive the baptism of "the friend of the bridegroom." Did Christ Himself baptise His own disciples before bidding them "baptise all nations." The Gospels do not tell us, but so it may well have been. Baptism was more than once administered by a prophet to his followers. At His Last Supper Christ exemplified before them all those things they were to do "in rememberance of Him." So too may it have been with regard to the ritual of baptism.

The Irish-American priest-poet has painted Our dear Lord cooling His tired feet in the waters, in lines that are all the more lovely to us because we feel they truly express the thoughts of the Master's tender heart.

"He walked beside the sea : He took His sandals off
To bathe His weary feet in the pure, cool wave—
For He had walked across the desert sands
All day long—and as He bathed His feet
He murmured to Himself, 'Three years, three years
And then, poor feet, the cruel nails will come
And make you bleed, but that blood will lave
All weary feet on all their thorny ways.'"

Father Ryan has in no whit exaggerated here. It was the Master Himself who let slip the words to the then uncomprehending ears of the Twelve: "I have a baptism wherewith to be baptised, and oh, how am I straightened until it be accomplished."

. . . . .

Round about us are the flowers that He loved, red flaming poppies, yellow mustard plants, white briar roses, red anemonies, oleander and cactus blossoms—all these are natives of Judea; flowers, "the sweetest thing God ever made and forgot to put a soul into." Just once in the Gospel do we get a picture of Him pausing in His speech to bid His disciples "consider the lilies": once only are these His words recorded, but the swiftness o fthe comparison, the loveliness of the language, could only come from one who had pondered long and lovingly over the exceeding fairness of these wayside blossoms. The illustration is so natural, it seems so inevitable when once it has been made, that it betrays an attitude of mind which must have been habitual. Were it some sudden revelation, some first appreciation of the glory "that doth so clothe the grass of the field," the comparison might have been equally touching but the language had not been so perfect in its fairness. The words that clothe new born thoughts have a something about them that lacks the ease and grace with which familiarity mates thought and expression. The haunting melody of Christ's words betrays no such ill-suited novelty. "Consider the lilies how they grow; they toil not neither do they spin, yet I say unto you not even Solomon in all his glory was arrayed as one of these." And yet natural though such a reflection be it is a foolish one to make. The least of Christ's words—I speak as one less wise—was as premeditated as the greatest, for it was the word of God made Man. Were these words then a familiar echo of early words of His which His mother had hidden in her heart, words spoken by the Boy in the little red-roofed home in Nazareth as He stood before her,

His hands clasping lovingly the wild flowers
He had gathered for her in the dew-drenched
fields around; not bunched together as the
dear, clumsy fingers of boyhood bind flowers
that touch many a mother heart, but trailing
their tender foliage in rippling cascades of
delicate beauty as the artist fingers of their
Maker alone could group them. Was it only in
the calix of the flowers that the dew diamonds
glistened, or were the loving eyes of the
Mother of God wet too, as humbly and
lovingly she took the blossoms, gazing down
the while into the little flower-face that was
lifted to her own? "Consider the lilies how
they grow." Flower of the field we thank
Thee for Thine own sweet loveliness. Draw
us that we may run after the odour of Thy
perfumes!

. . . . .

There would be no ending if we would
touch upon one half the things around us
that tell tales of His dear human life. The
stones, the mountain rocks spoke to Jesus of
Peter, His inconstant rock with his impetuous

loving heart, his dear human frailty. He saw the corn grow to maturity in the fields around His early home. He marked its progress: first the blade with its silken spear of tender green, then the pale tasselled ear whose sheath held naught but promise, last of all the full ear of corn kissed by the Judean sun to burnished silver—hence the fields there are *white* to the harvest—heavy with bread for the multitude that perished by the wayside. He saw the sower scatter the seed over the brown furrowed land, and marked the birds that followed in the train of the figure enveloped in the white grain sheet. He noted with loving care the birds—even the saucy rusty-coated sparrow, bickering and chattering then as now, birds that whisper of Our Heavenly Father's care for the falling bird, and for the man whose feet are upheld from the dark abyss by the hands of white-stoled Angels.

How tenderly the Boy Christ watched the sights familiar to every country child, how indelibly were they engraven upon the ivory tablets of His memory. He saw the brown speckled hen with her brood of fluffy, yellow chicks clustering round her, on her back, under her feet, struggling, jostling to get safely under the warm down of her wings, the same sight that fascinated your childhood and mine, beloved. But now that we have put aside the things of a child can we re-see it without memory calling up for us the pendent picture of the dear sad figure silhouetted by the sinking sun on the hillside that overlooked Jerusalem. "Jerusalem! Jerusalem, thou that stonest the prophets, how often would I have gathered thy children as a hen doth her chickens under her wings and thou would'st not!" Francis Thompson speaks of swinging the earth a trinket to his wrist, and lightly does the vast tellurian trinket hang from the frail emaciated hands of the starving outcast of the London streets, but here it is the Creator of heaven and earth who has bound for ever the colossal thought of His mighty tenderness to one of the weakest common sights of earth, even to a mother bird and her brood. Gather me, O Lord, under the shadow of Thy wings and keep me there for aye.

We can catch glimpses of the life of Our Lord in many of the daily household events of life; in the mother making bread for her family, hiding the leaven in the measure of meal. Many a Judean housewife must He have seen busy at such necessary occupation. Little would she have thought of what the thoughts were that stirred the depths of those grave all-seeing eyes, thoughts which but rested upon the Seen, from thence to take swifter flight to the Unseen. We find Him in the little accidents of life, in the anxiety attendant on the poor woman's loss of one coin or some other trivial necessary, in the care with which the house is swept and searched, in the joy that rewards the diligent searcher. The guest who puts hospitality into a generous panic by his unexpected arrival tells us that such happenings crossed Christ's path else whence took He His illustration of the importunate man who disturbed his neighbour at midnight for bread for his friend. Christ is here, He is there, He is everywhere in our daily lives for those of us who have eyes to see.

> Christ before me—Christ behind,
> Christ alone my heart to bind,
> Christ beneath me, Christ above,
> Christ around with Arms of love,
> Christ on all who look on me,
> Christ on every face I see.
> Christ on all who on me think,
> Christ their food and Christ their drink,
> Christ on all whom my thoughts seek
> Christ, the lowly, Christ, the meek.
> Christ in chariot, fort and ship,
> Christ to hold when anchors slip,
> Christ on all who list to me,
> May their ears hear naught but Thee.[1]

. . . . .

If we will we can find Christ in the books we read. We may or may not find Him in spiritual books. It all depends on how we read them. When we read a biography do we pass from the copy to the Model, do we

---

[1] Adapted from "The Breastplate of St. Patrick."

gather together the myriad rainbow lights of heaven into the one white Light par excellence, or are we only foolish stragglers who do not see the forest for the trees, who do not pass from the example to the meaning? Do we pause from time to time in our reading to look at Him, to ask what His message is *to us here and now?* If so be we read then we read aright, but we can find Him in secular books too, that is if there be anything secular but sin. Tales of chivalry show us only a pale reflex of His spirit, but a reflex at least shadows its original. We read of the Douglas who vowed to his dying master Robert Bruce that he would carry his dead heart into the wars and fight the enemies of Christ in his king's name, under his loved allegiance. Faithfully did the Douglas keep his vow, the chroniclers tell us, for whenever he met the Saracen he flung the treasured heart of his leader right into the press of the foe that so he might urge his own spirit to desperation in the effort to recapture the relic. Well did the writer of the following lines know how to apply such incidents to the Master's cause.

"Press forward as Thy wont, heart of my King!
Though all around Thee sounds of strife may ring:
Though in the battle's heat Thy path may be,
Lead where Thou wilt and I will follow Thee!

Striving beneath Thine eye, my King, my God!
Treading the footprints where Thy feet have trod!
Thy banner cross in view, Thyself so near,
No shrinking can be mine, no thought of fear.

Wearied and pale art Thou, all scarred with blows,
And forth from many a wound Thy life blood flows.
Thy heart so true and strong has loved me so,
Thou hast not spared Thy life to crush my foe.

Then oh, for love like Thine, as deep and wide;
Courage to follow Thee close to Thy side!
Faithful to Thee in life, true to Thy call,
Beneath Thy banner's shade at length to fall.

To fall beside my King! oh joy, to feel
My love for Thee is sealed by death's strong seal!
Clasped in Thy loving arms no more to part,
Calmly to fall asleep on Thy pierced heart!

We may find Him in the love of the father for his little child exquisitely portrayed in so much that is most delicate in the better side of modern fiction. The trustfulness of the child, the tenderness and unselfishness of the parent there depicted, inevitably call up our Saviour's gentle " argumentum ad hominem!" " If you being evil know how to give good gifts to your children, how much more will your Father who is in heaven give good things to them that ask Him. There is one scene in a well known tale of this type whose pathos touches one to the quick. It shows us a father clasping his small son in his arms and whispering in answer to the child's protest that he wants no playmate of his own age, " Nobody but Mother and you."

" Ah, . . . , . . . , if only there was any possibility of your saying that a few years hence." Does our Heavenly Father ever utter some such wish when He hears the innocent, lisping prayers of some amongst His children, prayers which later years, alas, are to belie . . . . . . Even in the novel proper we can find His traces. In the unselfish love of these not impossible human hearts one for another, there is surely some rebuke for our calculating advances towards our Heavenly Lover; their passionate desire for mutual service offers surely some reproach to our sluggishness; their delight in one another's presence has surely somewhat to say to our coldness. Oh Beauty, ever ancient, ever new, too late have I known Thee, too late have I loved Thee—too little do I know Thee, too little do I love Thee. Noverim Te Domine, noverim me, for if I know Thee aright I must love Thee!

.   .   .   .   .

That we can find Christ in the larger issues of life need not detain us here, it is so obvious. In our friendships we can relive the life of the Divine Friend of whom the Evangelist could say, "Now Jesus loved Martha and her Sister Mary and Lazarus." Nay, even in our swift impulses to sudden friendship we may mirror the Heart of the Master if only ours is based on the truest much that is most delicate in the better side of modern fiction. The trustfulness of the child, the tenderness and unselfishness of the parent there depicted, inevitably call up our Saviour's gentle "argumentum ad hominem!" "If you being evil know how to give good gifts to your children, how much more will your Father who is in heaven give good things to them that ask Him. There is one scene in a well known tale of this type whose pathos touches one to the quick. It shows us a father clasping his small son in his arms and whispering in answer to the child's protest that he wants no playmate of his own age, "Nobody but Mother and you."

"Ah, . . . , . . . , if only there was any possibility of your saying that a few years hence." Does our Heavenly Father ever utter some such wish when He hears the innocent, lisping prayers of some amongst His children, prayers which later years, alas, are to belie . . . . . . Even in the novel proper we can find His traces. In the unselfish love of these not impossible human hearts one for another, there is surely some rebuke for our calculating advances towards our Heavenly Lover; their passionate desire for mutual service offers surely some reproach to our sluggishness; their delight in one another's presence has surely somewhat to say to our coldness. Oh Beauty, ever ancient, ever new, too late have I known Thee, too late have I loved Thee—too little do I know Thee, too little do I love Thee. Noverim Te Domine, noverim me, for if I know Thee aright I must love Thee!

.   .   .   .   .

That we can find Christ in the larger issues of life need not detain us here, it is so obvious. In our friendships we can relive the life of the Divine Friend of whom the Evangelist could say, "Now Jesus loved Martha and her Sister Mary and Lazarus." Nay, even in our swift impulses to sudden friendship we may mirror the Heart of the Master if only ours is based on the truest bond of amity, which is God. "And Jesus *looking on him loved him.*" Let us go further and make this human craving spur us to ambition that to us too the words may be addressed, "I have called you friends."

Christ was a Jew, and if ever there was a people in whom patriotism rose from a natural to a divine virtue, that people was surely the children of Israel. We have Christ's own words that it behoved Him to fulfil all justice, so that even if the Gospel were silent on this point we would know that Jesus must have been a patriot. To the patriotic Jew his native land was no mere piece of earth, however smiling, however beautiful, however fertile. From the beginning of the world never was land so personified, so idealised. "Virgin Daughter of Sion," it was so He styled her. How the faithful Jew mourned over her sorrows, her degradation, how he exulted in the glory that had been hers, how he anticipated the day when once again she would be crowned a queen among the nations. In vain shall we look for echoes of these Songs of Sion among the peoples of antiquity. Even among modern nations not many can compare with the Hebrews in the fervour of their patriotic ideal. Yet, one there is whose devotion to a long suffering country all through the dark night of her sorrow has many points of similarity with Judea. "Dark Rosaleen" is a sister queen to this "Virgin Daughter of Sion." We find traces of Christ's devotion to His native land all through the Gospel, traces even of an exclusiveness which would trouble us if found elsewhere than in the person of our Lord, to whose own good time we can leave the explanation if such He deigns to give us. "I am not come save to the lost sheep of the house of Israel." "Go ye not into the way of the Gentiles, and into the cities of the Samaritans enter ye not." Christ's heart was wrung with compassion—we have His own word for it—at seeing His poorer brethren led astray by interested agitators, political or religious. Our own hearts too should bleed for the multitudes led by blind guides and therefore destined to fall into the ditch. Jesus, *Son of David*, have mercy on us. Save, O Lord, save Thy people.

.   .   .   .   .

So many points of contact with Your blessed life, dear Lord, and mine, points that in times past I have missed.

> "But now
> The hours I tread ooze memories of Thee, Sweet,
>   Beneath my casual feet
>   With rain fall as the lea
>   The day is drenched with Thee,
>   In little exquisite surprises
> Bubbling deliciousness of Thee arises
>   From sudden places
>   Under the common traces
> Of my most lethargied and customed paces."
>   FRANCIS THOMPSON.

www.ingramcontent.com/pod-product-compliance
Lightning Source LLC
Chambersburg PA
CBHW051715040426
42446CB00008B/903